MINI PUZZLES

CROSSWORDS

MINI PUZZLES

CROSSWORDS

SUPER SPEEDY PUZZLES

SIRIUS

SIRIUS

This edition published in 2024 by Sirius Publishing, a division of
Arcturus Publishing Limited,
26/27 Bickels Yard, 151–153 Bermondsey Street,
London SE1 3HA

Copyright © Arcturus Holdings Limited
Puzzles by Puzzle Press

ISBN: 978-1-3988-3692-1
AD011801US

Printed in China

Contents

1

¹	²	³	⁴	■
⁵				⁶
⁷				
⁸				
■	⁹			

Across

1 Neighbor of Earth

5 Archaic expression of dismay

7 Bête ___

8 Showing too much curiosity

9 Lawyers' charges

Down

1 "Dr. Faustus" author

2 Standoffish

3 Bring up

4 Stony hillside

6 Lock openers

2

Across

1 Mornings, initially

4 Butterfly's cousin

6 Defendants' entries

8 Listening organs

9 Six-sided roller

Down

1 Concert prop: abbr.

2 Blemish

3 Word with farm or home

5 Mata ___

7 Chicago to Miami dir.

3

Across

1 My, in Marseilles

4 Lively social event

5 Health, in France

6 Ash and oak

7 Vet's visitors

Down

1 "The Absinthe Drinker" painter

2 Rob of "Melrose Place"

3 "___ a Lady" (Tom Jones hit)

4 Unadorned

5 Fuel additive brand

4

1	2	3		
4			5	6
7				
8				
		9		

Across

1 Bad ___, German spa

4 Cook in the oven

7 "Tiny Bubbles" singer: 2 wds.

8 Firefighter Red

9 Org. with a caduceus logo

Down

1 "Das Rheingold" goddess

2 Emotional state

3 Yemen's capital

5 Adjust with a wedge

6 When said three times, a W.W. II film

5

Across

1 "Angels Like You" singer Cyrus

6 Soothsayer

7 J.C. Penney rival

8 "___ do" (answer to "No you don't"): 2 wds.

9 Defeated at chess

Down

2 "___ Darkness" (Johnny Cash song): 3 wds.

3 Minimal

4 Chill-inducing

5 Decade divs.

7 Orchestral composition: abbr.

6

Across

1 Woody Herman's "___ Autumn"

4 Coax

6 Opposite of "lower"

7 Microscopic

8 Antiquity, in antiquity

Down

1 Conical tent

2 Urge forward

3 Shell out

4 Ancient Egypt's King ___, for short

5 Have a go at

7

1	2	3		
4			5	6
7				
8				
		9		

Across

1 ___ nog, Christmas drink

4 Toot your own horn

7 Dazed and confused: 2 wds.

8 "I've ___ for music": 2 wds.

9 N.Y. org. that enforces alcohol laws

Down

1 Abba ___ of politics

2 Head for: 2 wds.

3 Neon and argon, e.g.

5 Close, as an envelope

6 Reid of "American Pie"

8

Across

1 Three-hand card game

5 Use elbow grease on

6 What a plane or ship carries

7 Hawadax Island resident

8 In the vicinity of

Down

1 Dieter's device

2 Seoul's home

3 Prophesy

4 Pony's pace

5 Scrutinize

9

1	2	3	4	
5				6
7				
8				
	9			

Across

1 Rescue

5 Error's partner

7 Major artery

8 Breakfast item

9 Lady of La Paz

Down

1 Near-random guess

2 "We're on ___ to nowhere" (Talking Heads lyric): 2 wds.

3 Sign between Leo and Libra

4 Devoured

6 "___ Land" (2016 movie): 2 wds.

10

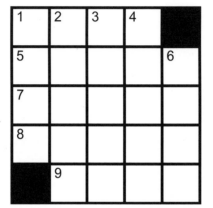

Across

1 Large brown seaweed

5 ___ Empire (online city-building game): 2 wds.

7 Dentist's tool

8 The duck in "Peter and the Wolf"

9 Take it easy

Down

1 Sneakers brand

2 Mistake

3 Jazz singer Cleo

4 City state in ancient Greece

6 Lacking points of prominence

11

¹	²	³	⁴	⁵
⁶				
⁷				
⁸				
⁹				

Across

1 Las Vegas area, with "The"

6 Stood

7 Greek physician and anatomist (129–199)

8 Hurt

9 Plant stalks

Down

1 Heroic tales

2 Inherited characteristic

3 Esther of TV's "Good Times"

4 "___ to recall…": 2 wds.

5 Awaits judgment

12

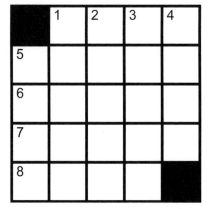

Across

1 Wetlands

5 Editor's mark, sometimes

6 "Blame It on Me" singer Davis

7 Introvert

8 Loads

Down

1 Bear in "The Jungle Book"

2 Praying figure

3 Inheritance controllers

4 Night light

5 Phone

13

Across

1 Singapore setting

5 Solid nourishment

6 Monopoly railroad: 3 wds.

8 Brandon ___, boxer nicknamed "Bam Bam"

9 Levelheaded

Down

1 Mil. jet locale

2 Flies high

3 Ancient Aegean land

4 Attach: 2 wds.

7 Suffix for sugars, in chemistry

14

Across

1 Metal shelf at the side of a fireplace

4 "___ Theme" (tune from "Doctor Zhivago")

6 Make happy

7 Broad valleys

8 "___ Miserables"

Down

1 Label for Muslim meat dealers

2 Vatican vestment

3 "Psycho" motel

4 Was in front

5 French pronoun

15

1	2	3	4	
5				
6				7
	8			
	9			

Across

1 Hope and Dole

5 City on the Oka

6 S. African village surrounded by a stockade

8 Analogy words: 2 wds.

9 Restrain

Down

1 ___ choy

2 Fragrant rootstock used in perfumes

3 Brute

4 Shade of gray

7 Actor Herbert of "The Pink Panther Strikes Again"

16

Across

1 Trims, as a tree

5 Egyptian peninsula

6 Toll

7 Unsuitable

8 Torme and Brooks

Down

1 Swedish taxonomist Carl von ___

2 Shaquille or Tatum

3 Spider's sense organs

4 Riverbed deposit

5 Thin layer on the surface of a liquid

17

1	2	3	4	5
6				
7				
8				
9				

Across

1 Brooklyn's ___ Island

6 Lyric poem written in couplets

7 Tractor-trailers

8 "Slow down, it's not ___": 2 wds.

9 Goes off on a tirade

Down

1 Romero who played the Joker on "Batman"

2 Drama set to music

3 "___ is an island": 2 wds.

4 Pronouncement

5 Toadies' replies

18

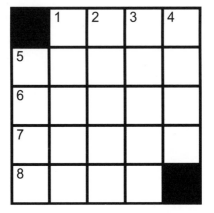

Across

1 Everest and Matterhorn, briefly

5 Soft and sticky

6 Firth of Clyde island

7 Dull photography finish

8 Pro votes

Down

1 Eel with sharp teeth

2 Bakery product

3 ___-foot oil

4 "Auld Lang ___"

5 Portuguese explorer Vasco da ___

19

Across

1 Mining surveyor's nail

5 Goalie Vokoun of the NHL

7 Angry

8 Actress Zellweger

9 Mont. neighbor

Down

1 Hubbub

2 Skin openings

3 Appliance brand

4 Palm fruits

6 Hunt for

1	2	3		
4			5	6
7				
8				
		9		

Across

1 Commercials: abbr.

4 Dry Italian white wine

7 Soothe, as fears

8 Calvin of the PGA

9 Lottery-running org., once

Down

1 Pronto, in office lingo

2 Hand (out)

3 Cut-price events

5 Brewery equipment

6 Storm centers

21

Across

1 Afternoon gathering

4 Take out ___ (do some borrowing): 2 wds.

6 Nasal partitions, e.g.

7 Leg joints

8 Gas: prefix

Down

1 Sun hat

2 Picky ___ (person who's tough to cook for)

3 Santa ___ (hot winds)

4 Try to get an answer

5 Songstress Horne

22

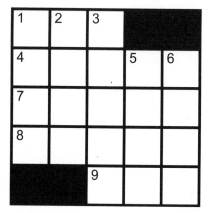

Across

1 Network with the Eyemark logo

4 A heap

7 "Kate & ____"

8 Silas of the Continental Congress

9 Family member

Down

1 Attired

2 Tree trunk

3 Light lunch

5 "Living Lohan" star

6 Word after sesame or poppy

Across

1 Small amount

4 La ___ opera house

6 Kitchen implement

7 Remove data

8 German's "the"

Down

1 Gogol's "___ Bulba"

2 Brewpub choices

3 Challenge

4 Went too fast

5 "Stranger Things" costar Buono

24

Across

1 File folder feature

4 "The Sabbath" painter Chagall

5 Composer Saint-___

6 Capital of Norway

7 Neighbor of Ill. and Mich.

Down

1 Asian weight units

2 The New Yorker cartoonist Peter

3 College football ranking format: inits.

4 Actor Oka of "Hawaii Five-0"

5 Farm female

25

Across

1 300, to Nero

4 Feel concern

5 Hackneyed

6 Love god

7 Gives a new color to

Down

1 Creek transport

2 Hardly refined

3 Cartoon collectible

4 Actor Grant

5 Four-poster, for example

26

1	2	3	4	5
6				
7				
8				
9				

Across

1 Line of cliffs

6 Piano fixer

7 "You ___ Beautiful" (Cocker hit): 2 wds.

8 Worn out

9 Acts as an usher

Down

1 Sports figures

2 1911 Chemistry Nobelist

3 End of ___: 2 wds.

4 VCR button

5 Digs into

¹	²	³	⁴	■
⁵				⁶
⁷				
⁸				
■	⁹			

Across

1 "The Cosby Show" boy

5 Ehud of Israel

7 "___ Zulu"

8 Eucharistic plate

9 Sound measure

Down

1 Cook's meas.

2 Lots of laughs: hyph.

3 One of the nine Muses

4 "The Old ___ Bucket" (Woodworth poem)

6 "Citizen ___"

28

1	2	3	4	5
6				
7				
8				
9				

Across

1 Joe of "Hill Street Blues"

6 You can see through them

7 Puts up

8 Stage whisper

9 Painter's plaster

Down

1 Mine roof prop

2 Bel ___ cheese

3 Avant-garde novelist Nin

4 Jocks' counterparts

5 Bone: prefix

29

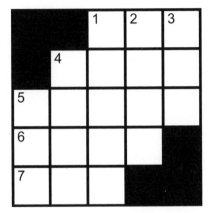

Across

1 Brick carrier

4 Pop singer Amos

5 Advances of cash

6 Fairy tale villain

7 Zeus or Poseidon

Down

1 Stockpile

2 River of northern France

3 Show no respect for, slangily

4 Like some pizza orders: 2 wds.

5 Cabin material

30

Across

1 Vincent van ___ (painter of "Irises")

5 Like Niagara Falls

7 "Edges" novelist Skolkin-Smith

8 Burdened

9 First name in 1950s TV comedy

Down

1 Chutzpah

2 Mountain nymph

3 "As the World Turns" actress Elena

4 Rabbits' cousins

6 Indian royal

31

Across

1 Weep uncontrollably

4 Unit of capacitance

6 Having wings

7 Dehydrates

8 Club ___ (vacation resort Co.)

Down

1 Beaver State capital

2 "___ Ben Jonson" (inscription on a tomb): 2 wds.

3 "With ___ breath" (in great suspense)

4 Scale notes

5 ___ Moines (Iowa's capital)

32

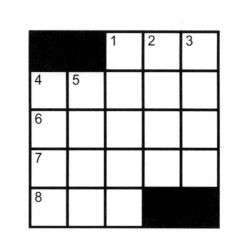

Across

1 Disallow to speak

4 Frighten

6 Change

7 Reagan aide Ed

8 Flier to Copenhagen, initially

Down

1 Movable barriers in fences

2 Greek god of war

3 "Pretty Woman" star

4 ___ Club (discount chain)

5 "The Alexandria Quartet" finale

33

Across

1 Hairless

5 Street show, old style

6 "Manhattan" and "Manhattan Murder Mystery" director

7 Visionaries

8 Curve of a ship's hull

Down

1 Bundles of straw

2 "Over the Rainbow" composer

3 Distrustful

4 Thieves' places

5 Dormitory overseers, initially

34

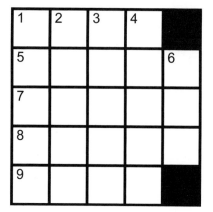

Across

1 Maori war god

5 Beside

7 "___ Books" (series written by Jacob Abbott)

8 Aviary sound

9 Beach, basically

Down

1 Chagall and Blitzstein

2 Hawaiian hello

3 1997 N.L. Rookie of the Year Scott

4 Lacking a guide

6 Republicans, initially

35

	1	2	3	4
5				
6				
7				
8				

Across

1 Quirks

5 Demi ___, actress

6 Burrell and Bancroft

7 Pigpens

8 Male bird

Down

1 Jay Silverheels role

2 Order of Greek architecture

3 Stream

4 Cong. period

5 Gender abbr.

Across

1 American ___, state tree of Massachusetts

4 Cooperative unit

6 Comedians Carvey and Gould

8 Ticked

9 Abbr. after some generals' names

Down

1 Approx. takeoff hr.

2 Pastoral expanses

3 Where the lord dwells

5 Filly's mother

7 Prepared

37

Across

1 Pianist Dame Myra

5 Falcon's home

6 Irish policeman

7 Native Canadians

8 When repeated twice, a "Seinfeld" catchphrase

Down

1 "Do I ___ Waltz?" (Rodgers-Sondheim musical): 2 wds.

2 Slipped up

3 Part of a single or LP: 2 wds.

4 Neptune's realm

5 Govt. group

38

Across

1 German trio

5 Cream soda brand: 3 wds.

7 Inscribed pillar

8 "Ready or not, ___ come!": 2 wds.

9 Disoriented

Down

1 Short run

2 Honey badger

3 January, to Mexicans

4 Sits around doing nothing

6 "Hold on!"

39

Across

1 Large mythical bird

4 Biblical son of Shem (Genesis 10:22)

6 Eric Dickerson was one, briefly: 2 wds.

8 Having a liking for

9 ___ Angeles

Down

1 Theologian's subj.

2 Patron saint of Norway

3 Yuletide song

5 Hand: Sp.

7 Rx prescribers

Across

1 Actor Arnold

4 Courted

6 Prefix with type

7 City on the Rhone

8 Gov. warning system

Down

1 Former Yankees manager Joe

2 Character in "Alley Oop"

3 Distributes, with "out"

4 New Deal prog.

5 Two, in Spanish

41

1	2	3	4	
5				6
7				
8				
	9			

Across

1 Food containers

5 Unhappy fan

7 Picturesque Ontario gorge town

8 Lets out

9 Harvest, as crops

Down

1 "Good buddy"

2 "You've got mail" message receiver

3 Who might be to blame: 2 wds.

4 Sealy rival

6 Woodworking tool

42

Across

1 Archipelago unit: abbr.

4 Abacus piece

6 Flowing tresses

8 Clothing designer
   ___ Jacobs

9 Cecil Campbell,
   a.k.a. ___ Kamoze

Down

1 Big name in servers

2 Dress feature

3 Porch named for a
   Hawaiian island

5 "The Great Gatsby"
   costar Bruce

7 ___-fi (literary genre)

43

Across

1 Belgian composer Jacques

5 Top-grade: hyph.

6 1980s–90s show with Jimmy Smits: 2 wds.

8 Tinseltown's Turner

9 Fender dent

Down

1 Bank account amount, briefly

2 "James and the Giant Peach" author Dahl

3 China's Zhou ___

4 "How Do I Live" singer Rimes

7 Jokester

44

	1	2	3	
4				5
6				
7				
	8			

Across

1 Measure of an economy, initially

4 Hen's hatchlings

6 Patronage

7 Makes progress

8 Vietnamese New Year

Down

1 "Super!"

2 Motherless calf in a range herd

3 ___ of law

4 Lunch holder, maybe

5 Grad. degree

45

1	2	3	4	■
5				■
6				7
■	8			
■	9			

Across

1 Paretsky of crime novels

5 Not that

6 "The Second Coming" poet

8 Dip ___ in (test): 2 wds.

9 Jardin Atlantique, par exemple

Down

1 Place for a pig

2 Lots: 2 wds.

3 Rope with a loop

4 Richest man on the Titanic

7 Short time, shortly

46

1	2	3	4	5
6				
7				
8				
9				

Across

1 San ___, Calif.

6 Dickens' ___ Heep

7 "SpongeBob Squarepants" lobster

8 British "19" singer

9 Organs of smell

Down

1 Disney movie of 1998

2 Plow, in Spain

3 Flags

4 Animation artist Eyvind

5 "I nearly forgot!": 2 wds.

47

1	2	3		
4			5	6
7				
8				
		9		

Across

1 Utah metropolis, initially

4 Warty amphibians

7 Hotel features

8 Charlie of "Hot Shots!"

9 Star Wars, initially

Down

1 Railroad buildings, briefly

2 Reluctant: var.

3 "Who ___?"

5 Expired

6 One-time bathroom brand, ___-Flush

48

1	2	3		
4			5	6
7				
8				
		9		

Across

1 Homer Simpson's dad

4 Loiters

7 Up ___ (trapped): 2 wds.

8 Roulette spinner

9 High-speed Internet inits.

Down

1 "There ought to be ___ !": 2 wds.

2 This one and that one

3 Like cornstalks

5 Lawyers' charges

6 Deal, trade

49

Across

1 Prompt (an actor)

4 Journalist Kupcinet

5 "Strawberry Wine" singer Carter

8 One who's coming out, shortly

9 Tokyo, once

Down

1 El ___ (Spanish hero)

2 Mary of "Where Eagles Dare"

3 Sidestep

6 Beatty of "Deliverance"

7 Blood-typing letters

50

Across

1 Kemo ___ (the Lone Ranger)

5 Gen. Robt. ___: 2 wds.

6 Water conduits

7 Way to go

8 ___ and buts, objections

Down

1 ___ Galilee: 2 wds.

2 Author's pen name

3 Curve

4 Suffix with employ or induct

6 Hosp. scanner

51

Across

1 Phrase of commitment: 2 wds.

4 Young horses

7 Musical Shaw

8 "Irons in the Fire" singer ___ Marie

9 ___ volatile (smelling salts)

Down

1 "___ first you...": 2 wds.

2 French illustrator of Dante's "Inferno"

3 Writer Joyce Carol ___

5 Filmmaker Wertmüller

6 Marine mammal

52

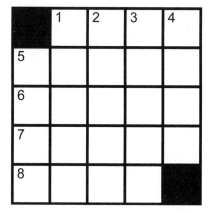

Across

1 Catherine who outlived Henry VIII

5 Pacific republic, capital Ngerulmud

6 Toy replicas of people

7 Gets away

8 Some kids

Down

1 Painter Veronese

2 "Manhattan Murder Mystery" director

3 Rapid series of short loud sounds

4 Pushkin's country, briefly

5 Some transmittable files, initially

53

1	2	3		
4			5	6
7				
8				
		9		

Across

1 Some ball-carriers: abbr.

4 Not held together

7 One year's record

8 "It don't ___ thing if it ain't got that swing": 2 wds.

9 Harry Potter's best friend

Down

1 Deception

2 Jolly Roger feature

3 Submarine detector

5 Healthy, in Spain

6 Verve

Across

1 Damage

4 G.I.'s mail drop

5 Denim pants

8 "Give ___ break!":
2 wds.

9 Wine classification

Down

1 ___ Gen.

2 Monkey's cousin

3 Goes here and there

6 Born as, in the
society pages

7 Cul-de-___

55

1	2	3	4	5
6				
7				
8				
9				

Across

1 ___ Novo (Benin's capital)

6 Zoe Saldana role

7 Ancient city in Egypt

8 Hint

9 Town and county in New York

Down

1 Glazier's need

2 Mitchell's Scarlett

3 Charge: 2 wds.

4 Instant

5 Desert watering holes

56

1	2	3	4	
5				6
7				
8				
	9			

Across

1 "Je ne ___ quoi"

5 "Up" star Ed

7 Golfer Palmer, to pals

8 Late fashion designer Geoffrey

9 A famous Scott

Down

1 Volvo rival, once

2 Comparable to a lobster: 2 wds.

3 Kind of tube

4 Le Havre's river

6 Marsh plant

57

Across

1 Flying mammals

5 Alpine river

6 Tangle

8 Hard-to-work-with type

9 Home of Zeno

Down

1 Some degs.

2 "Storage Wars" network: 3 wds.

3 Pursue

4 Start a tennis match

7 When doubled, a yellow Teletubby

58

Across

1 ___-kiri

5 Shipping weights

6 Frightful phantom

7 Lily family plants

8 Landlord's due

Down

1 Non-native, in Honolulu

2 Most common noble gas

3 Get a new tenant for

4 Enzymes' suffixes

5 One way up the slope: hyph.

59

Across

1 Web page addresses, initially

5 Drawing room

7 Rubberneck

8 Extend a subscription

9 Gets into

Down

1 Large nation letters, once

2 Assigned a rank

3 Grassy plain

4 Philosopher Kierkegaard

6 The latest

60

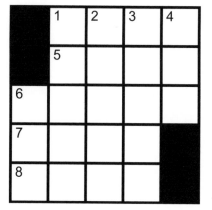

Across

1 Locality

5 Laundry batch

6 Compote fruit

7 Stringed instrument

8 Printing fluids

Down

1 "Yond Cassius has ___ and hungry look": 2 wds.

2 Family name in Frank Miller's novel "Sin City"

3 Noted Tombstone brothers

4 30-second spots on TV

6 Letter in some fraternity names

61

	1	2	3	4
	5			
6				
7				
8				

Across

1 Saudi, e.g.

5 Mrs. Dithers in "Blondie"

6 "Delphine" author Madame de ___

7 Brief and to the point

8 Publishing execs.

Down

1 Got on the stage

2 Engine sounds

3 Son of Zeus

4 Cotton unit

6 Sault ___ Marie

62

1	2	3	4	
5				
6				7
8				
	9			

Across

1 Condemn to hell

5 Columbus is its capital

6 Like the Vikings

8 Give a sign of welcome

9 Contributes

Down

1 Bell sound

2 Now, in Nicaragua

3 Bogged down

4 Pried

7 Little green men, initially

63

Across

1 Australian jumper, for short

4 St. John's ___, herbal remedy

5 Metrical feet in poetry

6 Winter ___ (flowering plant)

7 Native of Benin, Nigeria

Down

1 Rival of Paris

2 Eyes, poetically

3 Elevator pioneer

4 District

5 Diamonds, in slang

64

1	2	3	4	
5				
6				7
	8			
	9			

Across

1 Plays a part

5 Underground part of a plant

6 Rebound

8 Scarlett's plantation

9 Backyard structure

Down

1 Semicircle's shape

2 Paint layers

3 Religious scroll

4 Put in the pantry

7 Hot under the collar

65

	1	2	3	4
■	5			
6				
7				■
8				■

Across

1 Bird's bill

5 Hindu princess

6 Roots used in the Hawaiian dish poi

7 Ventures at the track

8 Tennis champ Arthur

Down

1 Scottish hillsides

2 Home planet

3 Win by ___: 2 wds.

4 "___ For Killer" (Sue Grafton novel): 2 wds.

6 Not yet decided, initially

66

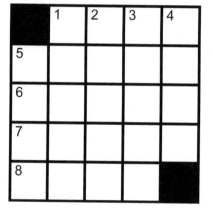

Across

1 Stationer's stock

5 Page number in a book

6 Numbers game

7 Make ___-ditch effort: 2 wds.

8 Greatly

Down

1 "Silent Storms" novelist Ernest

2 Place to exchange vows

3 Airheaded, informally

4 Chimney sweep's grime

5 Flavor ___ (rapper)

67

Across

1 ___-jongg

4 Jazz singer Vaughan

6 Deli specification: 2 wds.

7 Sycophant

8 Enjoyment

Down

1 "___ La Mancha" (musical): 2 wds.

2 Giant Amazon River turtle

3 Austrian composer, Joseph ___ (1732–1809)

4 Barfly

5 "___ Jude"

68

1	2	3	4	
5				6
7				
8				
	9			

Across

1 Pack animal

5 "It's just ___ those things": 2 wds.

7 Port town on the coast of the Sea of Japan

8 Goes on and on

9 Sci. class

Down

1 Sheep's coat

2 Like draft beer: 2 wds.

3 Dog restrainer

4 When life begins, some say

6 Bother

69

1	2	3	4	5
6				
7				
8				
9				

Across

1 Support

6 Humdingers

7 Muslim princes: var.

8 Gratis: 2 wds.

9 Salad green

Down

1 Highest Alp, Mont ___

2 It may be whispered

3 Common biography subtitle: 2 wds.

4 Fixes, as for illnesses

5 Curve shapes

70

Across

1 Firms: abbr.

4 Cut back

6 Public persona

7 Flower feature

8 Primus guitarist LaLonde

Down

1 Bedouin's beast of burden

2 Give a speech

3 E.C. ___, Sappo cartoonist

4 Spot on a domino

5 Dover's state: abbr.

71

Across

1 Pouches

5 Ensnares

7 Glowing remnant

8 Parenting challenges

9 "___ & the Women"
(Richard Gere
film): 2 wds.

Down

1 Leave-as-it-was notation

2 Having a weapon

3 Tossing the ___,
Scottish sport

4 Exhausted, as resources

6 They're older than jrs.

Across

1 Professor's degree, shortly

4 Sag

6 River joining the Rhône

7 More strange

8 "Peer Gynt" character

Down

1 "The Devil Wears ___"

2 Gangsters

3 Beneficiary

4 U.K. mil. award

5 Pay-___-view

73

Across

1 Calendar abbr.

4 Nat King ___

5 David ___, director of "Search and Destroy" (1995)

6 Prepare to propose, perhaps

7 ___ end (finished): 2 wds.

Down

1 Roman sandal

2 Comic DeGeneres

3 Banana skin

4 Defeatist's word

5 Jamaican pop music

74

¹	²	³	⁴	■
⁵				■
⁶				⁷
⁸				
⁹				

Across

1 Bacon, chicken and egg salad

5 "Here ___, there…" ("Old MacDonald" lyric): 2 wds.

6 "The Last Precinct" star Brooks

8 Canned meat rival of Spam

9 Smart-mouthed

Down

1 Farm vehicles

2 Actress Kate of "Dynasty"

3 Component parts of a skeleton

4 Augurs

7 Suffix with inferior or infidel

75

Across

1 ___-Mart (retail chain)

4 Bulgaria's capital

6 ___ di pollo (chicken breasts)

7 Have ___ (drink ale): 2 wds.

8 Word before Christmas or Pranksters

Down

1 "___ unto him who...": 2 wds.

2 Subsequently

3 Carafe size

4 Unwanted e-mails

5 Light and breezy

76

Across

1 Guy

4 Gave a hand

6 Idiotic

7 Airs

8 It comes after fah

Down

1 Without

2 "A Bell for ___" (1945 movie directed by Henry King)

3 Singer Cherry, whose albums include "Buffalo Stance"

4 River islet

5 "Der Ring ___ Nibelungen"

77

1	2	3	4	■
5				6
7				
8				
■	9			

Across

1 Seabird with a raucous call

5 Early mil. computer

7 Former BYU great Danny

8 Tennis great Federer

9 "Heartburn" author Ephron

Down

1 Equipment

2 Fusion, alliance

3 Local dialect

4 Bar selection

6 Michael of "Juno"

Across

1 Sandwich known by three letters

4 Song of triumph

6 Alpine ridge

7 Tennis champ Monica

8 Russian rulers of old

Down

1 Discloses

2 "Futurama" character with purple hair

3 ___ Tots (French fries alternative)

4 Over and done with

5 Fabled monster's loch

79

Across

1 Affleck and Stiller

5 African antelope

7 Bother greatly: 2 wds.

8 US flag features

9 Canada's ___ Island National Park

Down

1 Honey producers

2 Thrill no end

3 Area of South Africa, KwaZulu-___

4 Lewis Carroll creature

6 "The shakes," initially

80

	1	2	3	4
5				
6				
7				
	8			

Across

1 Junkyard dogs

5 ___ K., "Life in the Foodchain" singer

6 "Cheers" waitress

7 Short high-pitched sound

8 James Bond, e.g.

Down

1 Barbecue fuel

2 Turtle Bay VIP: 2 wds.

3 Life of ___

4 ___ opera (daytime show)

5 Letters in Aretha Franklin's "Respect"

81

1	2	3	4	
5				6
7				
8				
	9			

Across

1 Letter opener

5 Erga ___ (toward everyone, Lat.)

7 Baby grand, e.g.

8 Architect Saarinen

9 Was winning

Down

1 Blockhead

2 Oscar winner Jannings

3 "For want of ___, the shoe was lost": 2 wds.

4 Actress Taylor of "The Nanny"

6 Auctioneer's last word

82

1	2	3	4	5
6				
7				
8				
9				

Across

1 Sedate

6 Cocoon contents

7 Eastern

8 Musial and Laurel

9 "Steppenwolf" author

Down

1 Cut drastically, as prices

2 Try, like food

3 Opera songs

4 Several Russian tsars

5 "___ Macabre" (non-fiction book by Stephen King)

83

1	2	3	4	■
5				6
7				
8				
■	9			

Across

1 ___ the crack of dawn: 2 wds.

5 Rushed, as to attack: 2 wds.

7 ___ nous

8 Clothes-drying frame

9 ___ Grande, city in Arizona

Down

1 Common fertilizer ingredient

2 Lose one's cool

3 Natural cavities or hollows in a bone

4 Shipping weights

6 Prefix with byte

84

	1	2	3	4
5				
6				
7				
8				

Across

1 Hindu love god

5 Manages

6 Grating

7 Coeur d'___, Idaho

8 Caravan stopping points

Down

1 Australian "bear"

2 ___-ski

3 Intermediate, at law

4 "Angela's ___" (1996 best seller)

5 Rosalind of "The Joy Luck Club"

85

Across

1 Textspeak letters

4 Criticize in no uncertain terms

7 Roy Rogers movie, e.g.

8 Brother's daughter, say

9 Morse point

Down

1 "Off ___?": 2 wds.

2 Rapa Nui carvings

3 Like some communities

5 Dry, like Spanish wine

6 Old waste allowance

86

1	2	3	4	5
6				
7				
8				
	9			

Across

1 Spill

6 Illinois city

7 Old-fashioned "cool"

8 Women of distinction

9 Military cooks' assistants, slangily

Down

1 Mascara applicator

2 Spring ___: 2 wds.

3 Post office purchase

4 Lugs (around)

5 Seth's son

87

1	2	3	4	■
5				■
6			7	
■	8			
■	■	9		

Across

1 Just makes, with "out"

5 Chip's cartoon chum

6 Canonized person

8 Muscle quality

9 Tic-___-toe

Down

1 Publishers' hirees, for short

2 "Still Pitching" author Jim

3 "Silas Marner" novelist

4 Plant with laxative properties

7 Gumshoe, for short

Across

1 Cassette successors, for short

4 365 days, usually

6 Stuffs to the gills

8 Get into shape

9 Prefix meaning "within"

Down

1 Dermatologist's concern

2 "The Wreck of the Mary ___"

3 He tested Job's faith

5 "Sharknado" actress Tara

7 ___-Caps (candy brand)

Across

1 Great Salt Lake's state

5 Traveler's stop

7 Sports facility

8 King, queen or jack

9 Argentine aunt

Down

1 Thurman of "Pulp Fiction"

2 Ancient neck ornament

3 Really bothered: 2 wds.

4 Artist Toulouse-Lautrec

6 AvtoVAZ car brand

90

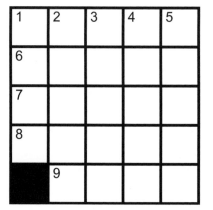

Across

1 Plus thing

6 Steplike part of a mine

7 Where Van Gogh painted "Sunflowers"

8 Archibald and Thurmond of the NBA Hall of Fame

9 Italian city with a leaning tower

Down

1 Saying: "… wise ___ owl": 2 wds.

2 Subway handhold

3 Conductor Georg

4 Fencing swords

5 Actress Ferrer of "Grey's Anatomy"

91

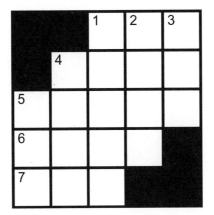

Across

1 Center of a peach

4 Gershwin's "The
___ Love": 2 wds.

5 Split ___ (quibble)

6 Composer of
"Rule, Britannia"

7 Drive-___ (quick
touring visits)

Down

1 Tony Bennett's
"Growing ___"

2 On the subject of: 2 wds.

3 "___ folly to be wise"

4 ___ Tyler Moore

5 Bible book before Zeph.

Across

1 Mo. after July

4 Be sick

5 Tailor's lines

8 "Drag Me to Hell" costar Dileep

9 Suffix with rep or rev

Down

1 Some batteries, initially

2 Road reversal, familiarly

3 Dazzling light

6 Calf's cry

7 Costa del ___

93

Across

1 "___ here" (ditto)

5 Lukas of "Rambling Rose"

6 Santa ___

7 Magnetic metal

8 Surrealist Magritte

Down

1 Part or portion

2 Moses' brother

3 Acadia National Park locale

4 That, in Spanish

6 Defunct space station

94

1	2	3		
4			5	6
7				
8				
		9		

Across

1 Neon, e.g.

4 Compounds capable of turning litmus red

7 ___ pedis (athlete's foot)

8 Acting award

9 Last part

Down

1 Cat, in Catalonia

2 Galatea's love in Greek myth

3 From that time

5 Campus V.I.P.

6 Variety of chalcedony

95

Across

1 Lash

5 Apartment agreement

6 Country rocker Steve

7 Color of envy

8 Academic terms, briefly

Down

1 "___ Family" (Sister Sledge album): 2 wds.

2 Women-only part of a Muslim household

3 The British ___

4 Hammer part

5 Lower limbs

96

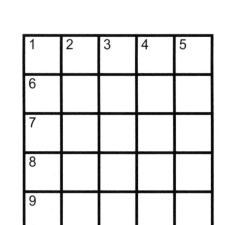

Across

1 Exposed

6 City in Parker County, Texas

7 Didn't take part, with "out": 2 wds.

8 Very slightly: 2 wds.

9 Wind-deposited soil

Down

1 Belonging to a bottom layer

2 Davy Crockett's last stand

3 Knot again

4 Prepares for press

5 Adores, with "upon"

97

Across

1 Group of related items

4 Angelou or Lin

5 Beginnings of some pranks

6 Historic times

7 Prince Valiant's son

Down

1 See-through wrap

2 "For Your ___ Only"

3 Prof.'s helpers

4 "Chloe ___" (A. A. Milne novel)

5 Narc's org.

98

1	2	3	4	5
6				
7				
8				
9				■

Across

1 Stage of development

6 Targeted

7 Flexible part of a whip

8 Afternoon in Acapulco

9 Suffix with social or suburban

Down

1 Rocker/poet Smith

2 Part of a drum set: hyph.

3 Dean Martin's "That's ___"

4 Puts in the mail

5 Border

99

Across

1 Unit of resistance

4 Vacuums

7 Long forearm bones

8 Sierra ___, mountain system

9 "America's Most Wanted" letters

Down

1 It can be fertilized

2 Greeting in Granada

3 "I don't ___ bit!": 2 wds.

5 Gloomy

6 "I ___ Dark Stranger" (1946 movie): 2 wds.

100

Across

1 Prepare to fire
  the cannon

4 What's more

5 Visit the land of Nod

6 Hopper

7 Little worker

Down

1 Make aware

2 "Now it's clear!": 2 wds.

3 Unruly mass of hair

4 Mathematician Turing

5 "___ boom"

101

Across

1 1300, in Ancient Rome

5 Palin from Alaska

6 Make up for

7 Eats out at a restaurant

8 Actors Bellamy
   and Eisenberg

Down

1 Monaco morning

2 Witchlike woman

3 Flogged

4 Bobby Fischer's game

5 Lamentable

102

1	2	3	4	
5				6
7				
8				
9				

Across

1 Fish usually caught in the winter

5 Forbidden by Islamic law

7 Spanish province or its capital

8 Ruckus

9 Like child's play

Down

1 Humiliate

2 "___ nice day": 2 wds.

3 Seed coverings

4 "Han Solo's Revenge" author Brian

6 West of Old Hollywood

103

Across

1 Chicago-to-Houston dir.

4 Overflow (with)

6 Glacial ice formation

8 ___ fide (law)

9 Tip for a pen

Down

1 Thoroughfares: abbr.

2 Appear to be

3 Linda Ronstadt album of 1998: 2 wds.

5 African nation

7 Subway alternative

104

	1	2	3	4
5				
6				
7				
8				

Across

1 "Drop this," editorially

5 Got by

6 Person born under the sign of the Ram

7 Actress Gray of "Dallas"

8 End of a winning streak

Down

1 "Deep Red" director, ___ Argento

2 Brockovich and Moran

3 Principal movie roles

4 "The Simpsons" teacher Krabappel

5 Drop to the ground

105

Across

1 Mafia leaders

5 "…and pretty maids all in ___": 2 wds.

6 Fort Knox measurement

8 Prefix with type

9 Belted out a tune

Down

1 N. ___ (st. whose capital is Bismarck)

2 Some grad school exams

3 Asian water-raising device

4 Steelers great Lynn who was the MVP of Super Bowl X

7 Dress up, with "out"

106

1	2	3	4	5
6				
7				
8				
9				

Across

1 Cold vegetable dish

6 Light ___ (insubstantial): 2 wds.

7 "Who's there?" reply: 2 wds.

8 Woodland plants

9 The Underworld, to Ancient Greeks

Down

1 Said, once

2 Stars, in Kansas' motto

3 Used a surgical beam

4 Pop singer Mann

5 Clothe

107

Across

1 Sesame, olive or canola

4 Ed of TV's "Daniel Boone"

6 Fashion designer Donna

8 Ice cream parlor item

9 "This ___ test…": 2 wds.

Down

1 Furniture wood

2 Innovative Apple computer

3 "Everybody Hates Chris" co-creator Ali

5 Minus in Marseille

7 Teacher's org.

108

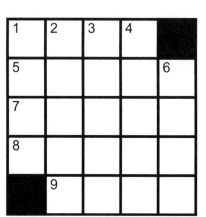

Across

1 Banda ___ (Sumatran city)

5 Fancy parties

7 "I can't believe I ___ much!": 2 wds.

8 Mexican mister

9 Long-winded tirade

Down

1 Turkish generals

2 Provide the meals for

3 "Uncle Vanya" woman

4 Is wearing: 2 wds.

6 Kind

109

Across

1 Sundry: abbr.

5 Class for foreigners, initially

6 "I ___ Man Like You" (Hugh Laurie song): 2 wds.

8 Run up ___ (pay later): 2 wds.

9 Middle of an apple

Down

1 "Who cares?"

2 Sci-fi author Asimov

3 ___ voce: softly

4 Unclouded

7 Honest ___ (Lincoln)

110

1	2	3	4	5
6				
7				
8				
9				

Across

1 Roast slightly

6 Cheri formerly of "SNL"

7 "A Tree Grows in Brooklyn" family name

8 Related on one's mother's side

9 Male and female

Down

1 Loaves of corn bread

2 In agreement: 2 wds.

3 Chill, so to speak

4 Prepare for shipping

5 "10 Days in a Madhouse" director Timothy

111

	1	2	3	
4				5
6				
7				
	8			

Across

1 Phone co. that merged with Bell Atlantic

4 Clean a ship's bottom, in a way

6 Cowboy's companion

7 Determined container weight

8 Classical pianist Anton

Down

1 React to a pun

2 Land in Lille

3 Artist's stand

4 All-natural food no-no, initially

5 It's not quite lge.

112

Across

1 Doesn't shut up

5 Type of lily

6 Win by ___ (barely beat): 2 wds.

7 "China Beach" actress Concetta

8 Pedal digits

Down

1 Google alternative

2 "That's ___ excuse!": 2 wds.

3 Works steadily at (one's trade)

4 Draped dress

5 Suffragist Carrie Chapman ___

113

1	2	3	4	5
6				
7				
8				
9				

Across

1 Business groups

6 Take ___ (don't stand): 2 wds.

7 "The Italian Job" actor Michael

8 Parisian aunt

9 Pacific, for one

Down

1 De ___ (in effect)

2 Biblical patriarch

3 Queen of France

4 Kind of ray

5 "The World Upside-down" artist Jan

114

1	2	3	4	
5				6
7				
8				
	9			

Across

1 Open ___ of worms: 2 wds.

5 NFL cofounder George

7 Web

8 Grunts like a pig

9 Russia's Itar-___ news agency

Down

1 Facetious "I see": 2 wds.

2 "Not another word!": 2 wds.

3 TV's "The George & ___ Show"

4 DEA figures: var.

6 Meeting: abbr.

115

Across

1 America, initially

4 ___ Wallace, "Pulp Fiction" character

5 "I Once Loved ___" (Scottish folk song): 2 wds.

7 Undergrad degrees, initially

8 Alliance that includes Azerbaijan, Armenia, etc.

Down

1 New England sch., home of the Minutemen: 2 wds.

2 Close female relative: abbr.

3 "___ in alpha": 2 wds.

5 Christie's "The ___ Murders"

6 My ___, Vietnam

116

Across

1 Teri of "Young Frankenstein"

5 Treats often taken apart

7 Draws close to

8 Moth-___

9 "___ Song" (Bing Crosby hit)

Down

1 Missing

2 Zones

3 Rodeo rope

4 "Air Music" composer Ned

6 IRS identifiers

117

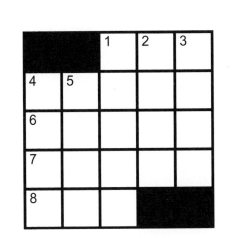

Across

1 Actress Ryan of "Sleepless in Seattle"

4 Have ___ (beware): 2 wds.

6 Chili con ___

7 Magician ___ Angel

8 101 instructors, briefly

Down

1 Niles's ex on "Frasier"

2 Sea eagles

3 The Bee ___ (singing group)

4 Billing abbr.

5 "Aimée Léduc" mystery writer Black

118

Across

1 Clay-lime mixture

5 "Hello, sailor!"

6 Club finance officer: abbr.

7 Richard of "A Summer Place"

8 H.S. diploma alternatives

Down

1 Homer's cartoon wife

2 Forward

3 Some horses

4 Fleur-de-___

6 Unshorn sheep

119

Across

1 Eczema symptom

5 Biblical mother of Boaz

7 Home of the University of Maine

8 Lines made of twisted fibers

9 Dick Tracy's love ___ Trueheart

Down

1 Dodge Daytona model of the early 1990s

2 Deck that includes swords, cups and coins

3 Unpleasant task

4 Arms' ends

6 Order (around)

120

Across

1 Space shuttle letters

5 Fortitude, informally

6 ___ Antoinette

7 One hundred dinars

8 It's under a foot

Down

1 Whodunit author Marsh

2 Ear-related

3 Steps that lead over a fence

4 Enzyme ending

6 Lady's title

121

Across

1 Keep ___ on (control): 2 wds.

5 Wearies

7 Actress Mitchell, Sister Robin on "Malcolm X"

8 Not so crazy

9 Detergent brand

Down

1 Down with, in France: 2 wds.

2 "Damn Yankees" vamp

3 Ryan of "The Beverly Hillbillies"

4 Dissuade

6 ___ Lee Corporation

122

1	2	3	4	5
6				
7				
8				
■	9			■

Across

1 Fairy-tale slipper material

6 ___-Wreck: hyph.

7 Excited

8 "Peer Gynt" composer

9 Currency of Japan

Down

1 Oldest boy on "The Brady Bunch"

2 City in Bowie County, Texas

3 1973 #1 Rolling Stones hit

4 Dutch painter, Jan ___

5 Marionette man Tony

123

Across

1 Biblical kingdom

5 Mediterranean island nation

6 Popular printing font

7 Canadian author Gallant

8 Currency of Western Samoa

Down

1 Charlotte Corday's 1793 victim

2 Minnesota Twins Hall-of-Famer Tony

3 "The Fox Without ___" (Aesop fable): 2 wds.

4 Light wood

5 Mother: var.

124

	1	2	3	4
5				
6				
7				
8				

Across

1 Go's opposite

5 Fugard's "A Lesson From ___"

6 Flattens

7 Aegean Sea island

8 "The law is ___..." (Dickens): 2 wds.

Down

1 Santa ___, Calif.

2 Exudes

3 Runs into

4 In ___ (existing)

5 Conquistador's chest

125

Across

1 Assay or essay, perhaps

5 More than dislike

6 Heart or liver

7 Cut down

8 Sense

Down

1 Number in a trio

2 Great Seal bird

3 Play for time

4 Lowest two-digit number

6 Not running

126

Across

1 Like two peas in a ___

4 Grizzly, e.g.

5 Exhausted

6 Lucky Charms ingredient

7 They're listed on birth certs.

Down

1 Bog deposits

2 Rower's pair

3 Like Chablis

4 Strike repeatedly

5 "Amazing!"

127

Across

1 The only even prime number

4 Cooked in hot fat

6 Lubricated

7 Secondhand

8 Not so much

Down

1 Bathroom squares

2 Garden invaders

3 Like 1, 3, 5, or 7

4 Free throw cause

5 Climb

128

Across

1 Cry from a crow's nest

4 God, to Muslims

6 "Mule Train" singer Frankie

7 Rainbow color

8 Objective

Down

1 County west of Tipperary

2 Extraterrestrial

3 Grew dimmer

4 North African nation: abbr.

5 Egg maker

129

	1	2	3	4
5				
6				
7				
8				

Across

1 Eliot Ness, for one: hyph.

5 Stiller's comedy partner

6 Wide selection

7 Beds for babies

8 Breaks a commandment

Down

1 One of the twins on "The Simpsons"

2 California county

3 Iranians and Iraqis

4 House votes

5 Apple computers

130

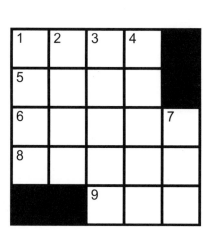

Across

1 1994 Jodie Foster title role

5 Snack item since 1912

6 "Te ___" (Gloria Estefan song)

8 Like a horse or lion

9 White stuff in Glasgow

Down

1 "Language and Mind" author Chomsky

2 Late humor writer Bombeck

3 Inclines

4 Sophia of "Two Women"

7 Child care expert LeShan

131

1	2	3	4	
5				6
7				
8				
	9			

Across

1 Cop calls, initially

5 Hand-operated implements

7 The Louvre, par exemple

8 Someone ___ (not yours)

9 "Little Man ___" (1991 movie)

Down

1 "You're Laughing ___" (Irving Berlin song): 2 wds.

2 Young fowl

3 ___ nova

4 Winter driving hazard

6 Zaire's Mobutu ___ Seko

132

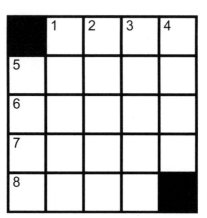

Across

1 French head

5 Underground worker

6 Tropical plant with straplike leaves

7 Loses moisture

8 Concluding

Down

1 Beauty queen's crown

2 City 35 miles south of Dallas

3 Article of faith

4 Pitching stats.

5 1450, to Cicero

Solutions

1

M	A	R	S	
A	L	A	C	K
N	O	I	R	E
N	O	S	E	Y
	F	E	E	S

2

A	M	S		
M	O	T	H	
P	L	E	A	S
	E	A	R	S
		D	I	E

3

		M	E	S
	B	A	S	H
S	A	N	T	E
T	R	E	E	S
P	E	T	S	

4

E	M	S		
R	O	A	S	T
D	O	N	H	O
A	D	A	I	R
		A	M	A

5

M	I	L	E	Y
	S	E	E	R
S	E	A	R	S
Y	E	S	I	
M	A	T	E	D

6

	T	I	S	
T	E	M	P	T
U	P	P	E	R
T	E	E	N	Y
	E	L	D	

139

Solutions

7

E	G	G		
B	O	A	S	T
A	T	S	E	A
N	O	E	A	R
		S	L	A

8

	S	K	A	T
S	C	O	U	R
C	A	R	G	O
A	L	E	U	T
N	E	A	R	

9

S	A	V	E	
T	R	I	A	L
A	O	R	T	A
B	A	G	E	L
	D	O	N	A

10

K	E	L	P	
E	R	A	O	F
D	R	I	L	L
S	O	N	I	A
	R	E	S	T

11

S	T	R	I	P
A	R	O	S	E
G	A	L	E	N
A	I	L	E	D
S	T	E	M	S

12

	B	O	G	S
C	A	R	E	T
A	L	A	N	A
L	O	N	E	R
L	O	T	S	

Solutions

13

A	S	I	A	
F	O	O	D	
B	A	N	D	O
	R	I	O	S
	S	A	N	E

14

	H	O	B	
L	A	R	A	S
E	L	A	T	E
D	A	L	E	S
	L	E	S	

15

B	O	B	S	
O	R	E	L	
K	R	A	A	L
	I	S	T	O
	S	T	E	M

16

	L	O	P	S
S	I	N	A	I
K	N	E	L	L
I	N	A	P	T
M	E	L	S	

17

C	O	N	E	Y
E	P	O	D	E
S	E	M	I	S
A	R	A	C	E
R	A	N	T	S

18

	M	T	N	S
G	O	O	E	Y
A	R	R	A	N
M	A	T	T	E
A	Y	E	S	

Solutions

19

S	P	A	D	
T	O	M	A	S
I	R	A	T	E
R	E	N	E	E
	S	A	S	K

20

A	D	S		
S	O	A	V	E
A	L	L	A	Y
P	E	E	T	E
		S	S	S

21

		T	E	A
A	L	O	A	N
S	E	P	T	A
K	N	E	E	S
	A	E	R	

22

C	B	S		
L	O	A	D	S
A	L	L	I	E
D	E	A	N	E
		D	A	D

23

		T	A	D
S	C	A	L	A
P	A	R	E	R
E	R	A	S	E
D	A	S		

24

		T	A	B
	M	A	R	C
S	A	E	N	S
O	S	L	O	
W	I	S		

Solutions

25

	C	C	C
	C	A	R	E
B	A	N	A	L
E	R	O	S	
D	Y	E	S	

26

S	C	A	R	P
T	U	N	E	R
A	R	E	S	O
T	I	R	E	D
S	E	A	T	S

27

T	H	E	O	
B	A	R	A	K
S	H	A	K	A
P	A	T	E	N
	S	O	N	E

28

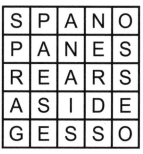

S	P	A	N	O
P	A	N	E	S
R	E	A	R	S
A	S	I	D	E
G	E	S	S	O

29

		H	O	D
	T	O	R	I
L	O	A	N	S
O	G	R	E	
G	O	D		

30

G	O	G	H	
A	R	O	A	R
L	E	O	R	A
L	A	D	E	N
	D	E	S	I

Solutions

31

	S	O	B	
F	A	R	A	D
A	L	A	T	E
S	E	R	E	S
	M	E	D	

32

		G	A	G
S	C	A	R	E
A	L	T	E	R
M	E	E	S	E
S	A	S		

33

	B	A	L	D
R	A	R	E	E
A	L	L	E	N
S	E	E	R	S
	S	N	Y	

34

M	A	R	U	
A	L	O	N	G
R	O	L	L	O
C	H	E	E	P
S	A	N	D	

35

	T	I	C	S
M	O	O	R	E
A	N	N	E	S
S	T	I	E	S
C	O	C	K	

36

E	L	M		
T	E	A	M	
D	A	N	A	S
	S	O	R	E
		R	E	T

Solutions

37

	H	E	S	S
A	E	R	I	E
G	A	R	D	A
C	R	E	E	S
Y	A	D	A	

38

D	R	E	I	
A	A	N	D	W
S	T	E	L	A
H	E	R	E	I
	L	O	S	T

39

R	O	C		
E	L	A	M	
L	A	R	A	M
	F	O	N	D
		L	O	S

40

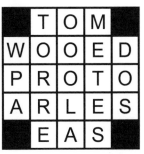

	T	O	M	
W	O	O	E	D
P	R	O	T	O
A	R	L	E	S
	E	A	S	

41

C	A	N	S	
B	O	O	E	R
E	L	O	R	A
R	E	N	T	S
	R	E	A	P

42

I	S	L		
B	E	A	D	
M	A	N	E	S
	M	A	R	C
		I	N	I

Solutions

43

B	R	E	L	
A	O	N	E	
L	A	L	A	W
	L	A	N	A
	D	I	N	G

44

	G	D	P	
B	R	O	O	D
A	E	G	I	S
G	A	I	N	S
	T	E	T	

45

S	A	R	A	
T	H	I	S	
Y	E	A	T	S
	A	T	O	E
	P	A	R	C

46

M	A	T	E	O
U	R	I	A	H
L	A	R	R	Y
A	D	E	L	E
N	O	S	E	S

47

S	L	C		
T	O	A	D	S
A	T	R	I	A
S	H	E	E	N
		S	D	I

48

A	B	E		
L	O	A	F	S
A	T	R	E	E
W	H	E	E	L
		D	S	L

Solutions

49

C	U	E	
I	R	V	
D	E	A	N	A
		D	E	B
		E	D	O

50

	S	A	B	E
	E	L	E	E
M	A	I	N	S
R	O	A	D	
I	F	S		

51

I	D	O	
F	O	A	L	S
A	R	T	I	E
T	E	E	N	A
		S	A	L

52

	P	A	R	R
P	A	L	A	U
D	O	L	L	S
F	L	E	E	S
S	O	N	S	

53

F	B	S	
L	O	O	S	E
A	N	N	A	L
M	E	A	N	A
		R	O	N

54

M	A	R	
A	P	O	
J	E	A	N	S
		M	E	A
		S	E	C

Solutions

55

P	O	R	T	O
U	H	U	R	A
T	A	N	I	S
T	R	A	C	E
Y	A	T	E	S

56

S	A	I	S	■
A	S	N	E	R
A	R	N	I	E
B	E	E	N	E
■	D	R	E	D

57

B	A	T	S	■
A	A	R	E	■
S	N	A	R	L
■	D	I	V	A
■	E	L	E	A

58

■	H	A	R	A
T	A	R	E	S
B	O	G	L	E
A	L	O	E	S
R	E	N	T	■

59

U	R	L	S	■
S	A	L	O	N
S	T	A	R	E
R	E	N	E	W
■	D	O	N	S

60

■	A	R	E	A
■	L	O	A	D
P	E	A	R	S
H	A	R	P	■
I	N	K	S	■

Solutions

61

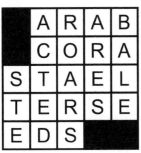

62

63

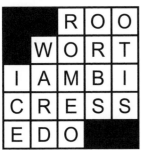

64

65

66

Solutions

67

	M	A	H	
S	A	R	A	H
O	N	R	Y	E
T	O	A	D	Y
	F	U	N	

68

W	O	L	F	
O	N	E	O	F
O	T	A	R	U
L	A	S	T	S
	P	H	Y	S

69

B	R	A	C	E
L	U	L	U	S
A	M	I	R	S
N	O	F	E	E
C	R	E	S	S

70

	C	O	S	
P	A	R	E	D
I	M	A	G	E
P	E	T	A	L
	L	E	R	

71

S	A	C	S	
T	R	A	P	S
E	M	B	E	R
T	E	E	N	S
	D	R	T	

72

	P	H	D	
D	R	O	O	P
S	A	O	N	E
O	D	D	E	R
	A	S	E	

Solutions

73

	S	E	P
	C	O	L	E
S	A	L	L	E
K	N	E	E	L
A	T	A	N	

74

C	O	B	B	
A	M	O	O	
R	A	N	D	I
T	R	E	E	T
S	A	S	S	Y

75

	W	A	L	
S	O	F	I	A
P	E	T	T	I
A	B	E	E	R
M	E	R	R	Y

76

	M	A	N	
A	I	D	E	D
I	N	A	N	E
T	U	N	E	S
	S	O	H	

77

G	U	L	L	
E	N	I	A	C
A	I	N	G	E
R	O	G	E	R
	N	O	R	A

78

	B	L	T	
P	A	E	A	N
A	R	E	T	E
S	E	L	E	S
T	S	A	R	S

Solutions

79

B	E	N	S	
E	L	A	N	D
E	A	T	A	T
S	T	A	R	S
	E	L	K	

80

	C	U	R	S
T	O	N	I	O
C	A	R	L	A
B	L	E	E	P
	S	P	Y	

81

D	E	A	R	
O	M	N	E	S
P	I	A	N	O
E	L	I	E	L
		L	E	D

82

S	T	A	I	D
L	A	R	V	A
A	S	I	A	N
S	T	A	N	S
H	E	S	S	E

83

U	P	A	T	
R	A	N	A	T
E	N	T	R	E
A	I	R	E	R
	C	A	S	A

84

	K	A	M	A
C	O	P	E	S
H	A	R	S	H
A	L	E	N	E
O	A	S	E	S

Solutions

85

O	M	G		
R	O	A	S	T
O	A	T	E	R
N	I	E	C	E
		D	O	T

86

W	A	S	T	E
A	L	T	O	N
N	E	A	T	O
D	A	M	E	S
	K	P	S	

87

E	K	E	S	
D	A	L	E	
S	A	I	N	T
	T	O	N	E
	T	A	C	

88

C	D	S		
Y	E	A	R	
S	A	T	E	S
T	R	A	I	N
	E	N	D	O

89

U	T	A	H	
M	O	T	E	L
A	R	E	N	A
	C	A	R	D
	T	I	A	

90

A	S	S	E	T
S	T	O	P	E
A	R	L	E	S
N	A	T	E	S
	P	I	S	A

153

Solutions

91

	P	I	T	
	M	A	N	I
H	A	I	R	S
A	R	N	E	
B	Y	S		

92

A	U	G		
A	I	L		
S	E	A	M	S
		R	A	O
		E	A	L

93

	S	A	M	E
	H	A	A	S
M	A	R	I	A
I	R	O	N	
R	E	N	E	

94

G	A	S		
A	C	I	D	S
T	I	N	E	A
O	S	C	A	R
		E	N	D

95

	W	H	I	P
L	E	A	S	E
E	A	R	L	E
G	R	E	E	N
S	E	M	S	

96

B	A	R	E	D
A	L	E	D	O
S	A	T	I	T
A	M	I	T	E
L	O	E	S	S

Solutions

97

98

99

100

101

102

Solutions

103

104

105

106

107

108

Solutions

109

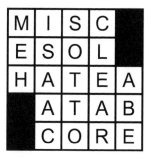

M	I	S	C	
E	S	O	L	
H	A	T	E	A
	A	T	A	B
	C	O	R	E

110

P	A	R	C	H
O	T	E	R	I
N	O	L	A	N
E	N	A	T	E
S	E	X	E	S

111

	G	T	E	
B	R	E	A	M
H	O	R	S	E
T	A	R	E	D
	N	E	L	

112

	Y	A	P	S
C	A	L	L	A
A	H	A	I	R
T	O	M	E	I
T	O	E	S	

113

F	I	R	M	S
A	S	E	A	T
C	A	I	N	E
T	A	N	T	E
O	C	E	A	N

114

A	C	A	N	
H	A	L	A	S
S	N	A	R	E
O	I	N	K	S
	T	A	S	S

Solutions

115

	U	S	A
	M	I	A
A	L	A	S	S
B	A	S	
C	I	S	

116

G	A	R	R	
O	R	E	O	S
N	E	A	R	S
E	A	T	E	N
	S	A	M	S

117

	M	E	G
A	C	A	R	E
C	A	R	N	E
C	R	I	S	S
T	A	S	

118

	M	A	R	L
	A	H	O	Y
T	R	E	A	S
E	G	A	N	
G	E	D	S	

119

I	T	C	H	
R	A	H	A	B
O	R	O	N	O
C	O	R	D	S
	T	E	S	S

120

	N	A	S	A
	G	U	T	S
M	A	R	I	E
R	I	A	L	
S	O	L	E	

Solutions

121

A	L	I	D	
B	O	R	E	S
A	L	E	T	A
S	A	N	E	R
		E	R	A

122

G	L	A	S	S
R	E	N	T	A
E	A	G	E	R
G	R	I	E	G
	Y	E	N	

123

	M	O	A	B
M	A	L	T	A
A	R	I	A	L
M	A	V	I	S
	T	A	L	A

124

	C	O	M	E
A	L	O	E	S
R	A	Z	E	S
C	R	E	T	E
A	A	S	S	

125

	T	E	S	T
	H	A	T	E
O	R	G	A	N
F	E	L	L	
F	E	E	L	

126

		P	O	D
	B	E	A	R
W	E	A	R	Y
O	A	T	S	
W	T	S		

Solutions

127

		T	W	O
F	R	I	E	D
O	I	L	E	D
U	S	E	D	
L	E	S	S	

128

	C	A	W	
A	L	L	A	H
L	A	I	N	E
G	R	E	E	N
	E	N	D	

129

	T	M	A	N
M	E	A	R	A
A	R	R	A	Y
C	R	I	B	S
S	I	N	S	

130

N	E	L	L	
O	R	E	O	
A	M	A	R	E
M	A	N	E	D
		S	N	A

131

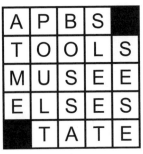

A	P	B	S	
T	O	O	L	S
M	U	S	E	E
E	L	S	E	S
	T	A	T	E

132

	T	E	T	E
M	I	N	E	R
C	A	N	N	A
D	R	I	E	S
L	A	S	T	